The WRITE State of Mind

13 Insights On Writing A Book From A Prolific Author

EMILY GOWOR

"I knew I felt called to write a book but I had no idea what to say or where to start — I was stuck. In our coaching, Emily weaved her magic to pull my topics out of me into an outline for my book. Because of her coaching and book outline, I wrote 60,000 words in just three weeks! Writing my first book and putting my thoughts on paper changed my life. Emily supported me through the writing and publishing of my book. I know she will draw out the best in you through her heart, soul and experience in writing many of her own books."

Deborah Toussaint

"Emily took me on a journey that I didn't believe I could go on until the end. Emily boosted my self-esteem and brought me to life again from inside. Thank you, Emily, for having confidence in me and telling me that I can do it. Because of you, I am the very proud author of I Still Call Zambia Home today."

George Masempela

"Thank you, Emily Gowor. Without your help, my inspirational journey would never have seen the light of day and, if it did, it would have just been another banged out book in the marketplace. With your help, it put so much more meaning behind my book and placed everything into more detail. You not only brought my book alive but every reader that has read it is absolutely loving it and I'm getting good feedback. Many people are thanking me for helping them change their perspective on life. I've sold it to all states of Australia and a few in the USA and the UK, too."

Lance Garbutt

"Emily is an inspiring book mentor. She helps me look at my writing in a different light, turning my book from a good idea into an incredible experience for myself and my readers. Her advice and guidance on my writing has been invaluable. She is a joy to work with – an asset for any budding author to help perfect a masterpiece!"

Jenni Reiffel, Entrepreneur & Author

"Working with Emily took me from disjointed writer to author within a matter of months. Her guidance, her methods, and her inspiration are invaluable tools to anyone wanting to maximise their inner creativity."

Simon Clark, Author of Shift Your View

"After having been in the very left-brain engineering profession for more than 20 years, I made the decision to leave and pursue a career in the personal development space. Part of my plan included writing a book. Emily was highly recommended, so I took up her services. The first great thing about this was that it forced me to write a synopsis of my book so that I had something to talk with her about. But what has been the most useful aspect of Emily's mentoring has been the coaching.

She is an incredibly wise and insightful young woman with more personal development experience and knowledge than most people twice her age. She has boosted my confidence and provided reassurance when I have had doubts or been struggling with procrastination. I would not hesitate to use Emily's mentoring again if (and when!) I start on a second book."

Haley Jones, Speaker & Coach

"With Emily's coaching, I wrote over 36,000 words in under 120 hours and created a revolutionary, thorough and science-based detoxification program. I am so grateful to you beautiful Emily, like a STAR that shone into a darkened room you have pierced through and switched on the creative juices within. I could not have achieved this without your inspired guidance. Thank you!"

Claudia Carmen Anton, ND

"I have had the good fortune to have been mentored on a regular basis by Emily Gowor. I have found her approach both empowering clear and practical Emily instils a deep belief in me for the words that I am writing. As she shares with me the impact my words have on her, I sometimes have to pinch myself that they are actually my words! I have never written a book before and through Emily's guidance and insight I have found this process to be a deeply uplifting and transformational experience."

Nikki Slade, Author of Free The Inner Voice

The Write State of Mind: 13 Insights On Writing A Book From A Prolific Author © Emily Gowor 2017

www.emilygowor.com

The moral rights of Emily Gowor to be identified as the author of this work have been asserted in accordance with the Copyright Act 1968.

First published in Australia 2017 by Gowor International Publishing

www.goworinternationalpublishing.com

ISBN 978-0-9945944-7-1

Any opinions expressed in this work are exclusively those of the author and are not necessarily the views held or endorsed by Gowor International Publishing.

All rights reserved. No part of this publication may be reproduced or transmitted by any means, electronic, photocopying or otherwise, without prior written permission of the author.

Disclaimer

All the information, techniques, skills and concepts contained within this publication are of the nature of general comment only, and are not in any way recommended as individual advice. The intent is to offer a variety of information to provide a wider range of choices now and in the future, recognising that we all have widely diverse circumstances and viewpoints. Should any reader choose to make use of the information herein, this is their decision, and the author and publisher/s do not assume any responsibilities whatsoever under any conditions or circumstances. The author does not take responsibility for the business, financial, personal or other success, results or fulfilment upon the readers' decision to use this information. It is recommended that the reader obtain their own independent advice.

Dedicated to the writer you are, the writer you can be, and the writer you will become as you share your heart and soul with the world.

*"You may not think you are a writer,
but when you have something important to say, you
will become one."*

Emily Gowor

Contents

Introduction 1

1: Find the book within you 9

2: Make a plan for your book 17

3: See great things for yourself 23

4: Writing is a sacred practice, so treat
    it like one 29

5: Focus on the message and the words
    will come 37

6: Unite your life with your book and your
    book with your life 45

7: Writing your book will change your life 51

8: Grow into your content 57

9: Your readers can feel you 63

10: Bear your soul on the page 73

11: You have an infinite well of content
     within you 81

12: Write for your readers 91

13: Focus on your long-term vision 101

Conclusion 109

Enrol in Retreat To Write! 113

About The Author 115

Acknowledgements 117

Additional Titles by Emily Gowor 119

Introduction

> *"We write to taste life twice; in the moment and in retrospect."*
> **Anais Nin**

My affinity with writing has spanned the length of my life.

The love affair began way back when I was a mere foetus in my mother's womb. She invested more than 400 hours reading to my older brother David. And so, while I was busy developing my body ready for life on Earth, I was already falling in love with words. Given the extensive amount of time I spent listening to and feeling the vibrations of my mother's voice as she told stories and taught my brother (and I) about the world, it is no surprise that I popped out with a determination to devote my life to all things words.

It is also no mystery to me why I often experience an overwhelming sense of unconditional love when I sit down to write. A little psychological analysis would likely show that I have a *powerful* connection between what it feels like to be loved (by my mother) and the world of words. When I write, I feel at one with life, I feel fed from deep within, and I feel that all is well in my world: that I am surrounded by everything I need.

(The thousands of hours of floating in amniotic fluid and being read to during my mother's pregnancy with me has also solidified my typically auditory learning style. I easily retain what I hear and can often reproduce it word-for-word at a much later date, complete with inflections and punctuation!)

The love affair developed into a stint of fiction writing as a child before stumbling into the world of poetry as a teenager (my way of soothing my inner angst). I tried my hand at a wide range of writing styles and forms before finding my authentic groove as a writer around age 17 in the topics of spirituality, inspirational content, and now, today, business writing.

Through the many phases of my journey as a writer, my appreciation and respect for the power of the written word and the seemingly simple act of writing has grown dramatically. Time and time again, I have found myself humbled by how intensely the act of expressing my thoughts and feelings on paper changes me: how it inspires me, how it shapes me, how it supports me, and how it nourishes my very being.

Writing has been central to my emotional wellbeing, a pathway for me to discover my true potential, a way for me to find what I hold dearest in life, and, as it turned out, the foundation of a thriving career bringing inspiration to the world. Without writing, my life would lack the abundantly deep meaning it has today and I would be unsure of the purpose for my existence.

This love of words that is now inextricable from my identity, sense of self, and connection to my greater destiny followed me into my career. After working in retail selling books (yes, I know! No mistake, right?) as a late teen, I was offered the opportunity to write an article about a social entrepreneur for XL Magazine. My connection there had noticed that I loved to write and believed that I could do more with myself and my future than work for $13 an hour. I wrote the article, it was published, and the connection referred me to another client.

My career as a paid writer had begun!

A long line of achievements followed as I found my feet in business at the young age of 19. One year later, I received an invitation to assist international best-selling author and speaker Dr. John Demartini, who I had been studying with at the time, in producing the first manuscript of his book, *Inspired Destiny*. I had entered the slipstream of what inspired me – words – and life was working with me to create greater and greater opportunities to share my gift (and love) with people.

Word got around that I was the go-to chick for people who needed help with articulating their message on paper. Soon, I was writing professional biographies for entrepreneurs and leaders, ghost-writing books for international speakers, and making my name as the 'Word Artist' – my first personal brand. The tagline stuck so strongly that people would introduce me as the Word Artist before they used my first name and friends began replacing 'Em' with this moniker.

It was out: the world knew that I was a writer... and so did I!

(If you flick to the Acknowledgements of Dr. Demartini's book, *Inspired Destiny*, you will see that even he used the term 'word artist' in his expression of gratitude for my contribution to his book.)

At age 22, I was offered the opportunity by a small-time publishing house based in New Zealand and Italy to be the author of an interview series, *Transformational Leaders*, where I would write the stories of 13 influential individuals across a range of industries from health and wellbeing to environmental causes. By age 23, I had achieved a childhood aspiration that I had only dared dream of: I had become a published author!

Introduction

The feeling was surreal – and it still is today. My publisher had secured more than $20,000 of sponsorship funding for the book through a multi-million-dollar company. This saw me launch my first book at their annual conference where I spoke in front of an audience of 250+ people two nights running. So, there I was, holding my first book in my hands before the age of 30.

The spark had turned into a roaring flame and I soon launched my career as a book mentor and writing trainer. Besides coaching hundreds of authors to bring their message from the head and heart to the page, I ran live events in Australia and delivered nine online author training programs in various niches of book writing (from memoir to how to produce a book from transcripts).

In 2013, I founded a self-publishing company – Gowor International Publishing – to serve the clients I had been coaching to start, write and finish their books. I spent four years expanding my repertoire in the book space to all parts of the publishing process. This included the exciting part of the author's journey where the book turns from a Word document into a book they can hold in their hands! In doing so, I further developed my natural creative flair for assisting authors.

In my career as an author, I quickly followed my first book by writing and publishing seven more books in the self-help and book-writing genre by the time I was 29 years old. I'd say the writing bug had bitten me, but I believe that happened long before the books made it into a published format!

For many years, I've spoken on podcasts and webinars, taught from the stage, created numerous training resources, and shared online to help other people master the art and experience the depth of joy I receive from the written word. This journey has continued to unfold and has now expanded into regular writing retreats, which provide budding authors the opportunity to write their book in a beautiful location with my full support.

Today, I very much feel it is an inherent part of my mission on Earth to inspire people to write their book, and to help them to overcome whatever it is – be it practical or psychological – that prevents them from communicating their important message for the world. It is a true privilege that I am blessed by on a daily basis.

My mission today? To bring inspiration and books to the world.

Everywhere I go, I meet people who want to write books, who have stories to tell, and who have been thinking about putting their knowledge onto paper, but who have struggled to start the process of doing so. I also seem, as if by magic, to attract people who have a world-changing message to share or a mission for which becoming an author is a high priority.

The likelihood is, if you are reading this, then you fit into *both* categories! And if this is true, then you are in luck because it is YOU for whom I wrote this book.

In this book, I will share 13 of the most powerful insights I have acquired on my writing journey to help *you* access the life-changing power of writing and, of course, bring out the book that is within you. I will take you on a journey into the psychology of a writer and provide you with valuable strategies and ideas to get into 'the zone' so you can produce thousands of words on demand whenever you need them, whether that is for your book, business or your life.

YES, this book is about how to cultivate the 'write' state of mind for the journey ahead!

It is as much about breaking through your blocks and fears as it is about me sharing my deep love of writing with you. It is about quietening the noisy voices and concerns that chatter away in your mind, pulling you away from and out of your writing flow. And, perhaps more importantly, it is about showing you just what is possible when you enter the 'write' state of mind.

So, strap yourself in... and let's begin!

1: Find the book within you

"There is no greater agony than bearing an untold story inside you."

Maya Angelou

So, you have an idea for a book. Congratulations, you've taken the first step towards becoming an author!

I say this with a light-hearted joy but also seriousness, because it is true that every book starts with just that: an idea. It's mind-boggling when you think about the millions of books that people have laboured over to bring into the world; every one of them began with someone who said, "I want to write a book about that", or "The world needs to know this." They each began with a thought, a feeling, a desire, a vision, a concept.

And then, through determination, strategy and (hopefully), inspiration, the idea began to take shape and form until one day the author could hold the book they'd envisioned in their hands: an experience that stays with you for life.

Yes, ideas for books are a dime-a-dozen (believe me, I've heard hundreds upon hundreds of book ideas in the past decade), but this doesn't make the ideas themselves less powerful or valuable. In fact, perhaps we skip too quickly past the moment where the book introduces itself to us in the form of an idea, a passing comment, a thought while driving, or a lightbulb revelation. It is *because* of the idea that the book even becomes possible: it is the spark for the flame, the seed for the flower, the acorn for the oak tree.

So, let's take a moment right now to simply *appreciate* that the idea for a book has graced your life with its presence – an invitation for you to write it, heal through it, publish it, and perhaps grow a thriving business as a result. And then, stop in reflection to acknowledge yourself for accepting that invitation and being willing to surrender yourself and become the vehicle for this book to emerge into the world.

Remember: most people have had an idea for a book at some stage in their life, but only a small percentage of people commit themselves fully to making the time, harnessing the patience, and taking the journey

1: Find the book within you

to see the book turn from that idea into a finished, published product.

Lives *will* be touched, moved and changed because of the book you are about to write and *that* makes YOU an invaluable individual in this world: a significant force waiting to happen, a guiding light for the lost, and a courageous leader bold enough to speak their truth for those who are willing to listen (or in this case, read!).

Now, once you know what the concept of your book is, you must ask yourself:

> "How much do I *love* this idea?"

The underlying motive for asking this question rests on my observation that the people who don't just begin their books but finish them and can call themselves an author are those who simply can't wait to write the book.

They don't just see the book as a shortcut to growing their business; they see it as a way to change the world. They don't just think the book is something they have to do; they feel it is part of their calling and destiny on earth to write it. And they aren't interested in banging out just any old content and slapping on a cover; they believe their manuscript is a masterpiece waiting to happen.

That is the kind of attitude that births world-changing books. The *only* way to write a book that goes viral and shares your wisdom and knowledge with millions of people is to write a book that has come from *within* you: a book that you LOVE.

Take this book for example: *The Write State Of Mind*. I'm writing this book to share my powerful world of writing with you and to invite you into the world of word-flow. I'm writing it to spread my inspiration for the written word so that the inspiration can be magnified, and people's lives can transform because of the book or books authors write. And I'm writing it because watching people tapping into their inner writer amplifies the deep meaning for my life ten-fold.

It's also worth saying here that my love for this book idea is so strong that I put another book on hold to allow this one to emerge first! It's not 'just a book' to me, and any rewards it brings me in business by further profiling me as a writing trainer is a secondary benefit: a flow-on effect, if you will.

The more you *love* your book idea, the greater your inspiration for writing it will be. The more you *love* your book idea, the more determined and driven you will be to finish it and share it with the world. The more you *love* your book idea, the chances of the book falling out of your heart and mind effortlessly onto the page will skyrocket. *And*, if you are writing your book for business purposes and financial gain through serving a wider audience (which, by the way, is not impure in any sense of the word), then the more you *love* your book, the more opportunities you will attract once you publish the book.

Your love is what *drives* your book, and without it, your book idea might just curl up and die.

If you've answered the question honestly and you can say *"YES, I love my book idea!"* and you can't wait to write it, then take a moment to imagine me yelling "WOOHOO!" or giving you a big thumbs-up! And if you've felt an 'uh-oh' because upon reflection you realize that this book idea isn't the one that lights you up from within, then don't fret.

I have had many a book idea come my way over the years, but I haven't written them all. I've let many go, surrendering them back to where they came from or even passing them on to other authors (perhaps the rightful writer for that book) who have taken the spark and run with it. I am sure that only a small percentage of all the things I know or feel I could write about will make it to the page in my career as an author – even if I spent my entire life doing nothing else but writing.

This doesn't make me sad: it makes me more present with and thankful for the ideas that land with me and do reach the bookshelf because then I know they are the *right* ones. The *right* book idea is the one that draws your knowledge out of you effortlessly, holds the space for you to express and heal yourself, and gives you an experience of awe and wonder at just how much you *do* know that can assist, change and impact the lives of the readers. In other words, it gives you an experience of just how truly incredible and infinitely brilliant you are. It blasts away the cobwebs of disbelief in oneself and replaces them with self-respect (which is crucial for creating an extraordinary life, no matter what your goals and aspirations may be).

So, the key here is to, firstly, remain unattached to your idea by trusting that there *is* a perfect book just waiting for you to write it. Plus, it is a book that, while being written by you, will shape you into a greater human being. Trust that you have a deep and infinite well of words, wisdom and truth within you and that the *right* book idea will not only bring these out of you, but blow your mind with its value as you write it.

Yes, I know it's tricky sometimes to let go of a book; perhaps you're afraid just to let it slip away and return to where it came from. But all my years writing books have shown me that if my heart's not in it, I will stall myself and avoid writing it, I'll run into writers' block, or I won't love the finished product, which is a colossal waste of my time and energy! It's just not worth the struggle when the book you're destined to write does exist and the moment you align with it, magic will happen.

(Sidenote: I'm certain that the authors who grip on to their idea too tightly sometimes prevent the book from evolving into what it is meant to be.)

1: Find the book within you

Once you have let go of your book idea (take one), turn your heart and head back to your life and the world around you. Devote yourself to a deep study of yourself and what moves you and commit yourself to further clarifying your vision for the future. If you do this and simply *trust* the process, you *will* meet the ONE! You will meet the book that yearns for you to write it and that you yearn to write, as I say, the book *within* you, not just a throwaway idea.

And that book? It's worth the wait!

2: Make a plan for your book

"Planning is bringing the future into the present so you can do something about it now."

Alan Lakein

Once you are armed for the journey – with your book by your side – it's then time to make a plan for your writing process.

What does this mean, you ask?

It means defining and designing what your writing journey will entail, and, more specifically, what plan you are going to follow to bring your book to life.

The question I am asked the most often by aspiring authors is: "How do I structure my content and organize my thoughts into a book?" Besides providing the emotional and spiritual encouragement and inspiration often needed to manifest a manuscript and take it through to the end of the publishing process, this aspect of the writing process is the one into which I am most commonly invited.

I get it: having what feels like a zillion ideas for what goes *in* your book – all the things you want to write about and feel belong as part of this published work – and trying to line them up can sometimes feel like herding cats. How do you know what goes where? Where should you start? How much do you share of your story? How do you choose the order of your content and teachings? What should you leave in or, indeed, leave out entirely?

These questions are extremely relevant to the process of writing well, and yes, they are normal. In fact, if you don't ask and then find answers for them during this next stage of writing a book – the book outline – then you may quickly find yourself tangled up in a mess inside a Word document, which can be incredibly disheartening, especially for a first-time budding author.

This isn't a phase that you can afford to skip if you want to publish your name on a manuscript worth reading and raving about. In fact, mapping out your plan for the book is crucial to the final completion of your project, not to mention its success once it has been published and offered to the world as a product.

2: Make a plan for your book

Sketching even a rough outline for your book before you touch pen to page (or fingertips to keyboard) will provide you with a plan to write to, an end goal to think about, and the blueprint for a book that is coherent for the reader. In a nutshell, it provides you with the foundation you need to start and finish your book and it keeps you focused on the all-important carrot of completion along the way.

If you *don't* take the time to plan what you will include in your book and in which order, you increase the likelihood of running into writer's block, where you sit and stare at your screen feeling lost. Or, you might end up feeling overwhelmed by the process and giving up on your heartfelt book idea entirely (which is crazy talk, as you can avoid this by making a proper plan!).

But if you do take the time to envision how and where you will write about your grand ideas? You can easily *halve* the time it would otherwise take you to produce your book. Not to mention, this will also put the ball in play for you to have an *extraordinary* and *life-changing* experience letting your teachings, story and content out onto the pages of your book.

I once spent five hours planning the outline for a book before I allowed myself to start the writing process. It was painful, as it felt like the book was bursting to come out of me. I was like a horse chomping at the bit! However, my discipline to hold myself back for just a few more hours rewarded me ten-fold, as I managed to produce a whopping 51,000 words of content for my next book in less than four days with relative ease. In addition, it was also one of the most rewarding encounters I have ever had with the written word.

I have coached thousands of authors and reviewed hundreds of books over the years, and I can tell you that there is a *stark* difference between the books that were written to a plan and those that were written without much thought. The latter usually end up as random content joined together in a Word document, whereas books that are written with a plan flow properly. Those that aren't planned don't flow at all, and in fact, most times they either bore or lose me completely.

Yes, I'm anally retentive about planning properly for your book before you begin but it's because I don't want you to drown in your thoughts while you try to fulfil your dream of writing a book and getting published. It's also because I know that you *do* have a best-selling book inside you and thus, the potential and capability to write one. But you'll need a plan to support you in achieving this grand outcome for yourself.

In my experience, most people set out to write a best-selling book but fall short of producing a manuscript *worthy* of hundreds of thousands of sales because they lack the patience necessary to think it through before they hit the ground running.

2: Make a plan for your book

The best books I have personally read – you know, the ones I couldn't put down and that I wanted to push everything else aside to read (oops, I nearly typed 'write'!) – are those with a clear outline. In such books, it's easy to see what is what, what is where, how to find the information you need, and which part of the book is which. The effort the author makes in planning can be noticed in the end product, as the structure of the content creates a journey for the reader to take as they read the book.

This creates flow in the reading experience and answers the reader's questions along the way so they aren't left with gaping curiosities about what you meant and how to apply your teachings to their life. Also, it supports them as they read from the first page to the final page, leaving them feeling deeply impacted as they read the final words of the conclusion and close the cover.

It's also worth saying here that pausing to produce a proper plan for your book will support you in writing a book that has consistent chapter lengths, author's voice, tone and energy: all significant keys to writing a book worthy of being a best-seller. By having a plan in hand when you sit down to work on your manuscript, you will maintain a clear picture in your mind of where quotes, topics and information should go. This will allow you to be more capable of seeing what else you can do to knock your book out of the ballpark.

Buddha said: "Teach them the illusion until they're ready for the truth." When applied to your book and the world of book writing, this simply means that you have given thought to what goes where in your book to optimize the reader experience.

Beyond this, well-organised content shows the reader that the author knows what they are talking about. It also sets the author up for speaking opportunities. Nearly all event organisers I have worked with want to know that the speaker can teach their content in a structured format onstage, using a microphone, to a live audience (waffling doesn't fare well in the speaking industry!).

The plan you set in place for your manuscript will also be a plan for you as, when done correctly, it can create the foundation for opportunities for programs, coaching systems, online blog materials, media articles, retreats and, yes, keynote speaking presentations.

So, if you want your book to be a *great* one – and you don't want the experience of writing it to feel like a form of torture – make sure you invest your time in making a plan for your book. It will reap dividends for your writing adventure in ways you can't even imagine.

3: See great things for yourself

"Believing that you have no purpose in this world is like believing that the flowers need no sunshine."

Emily Gowor

I believe it is anything but a random act of life that you are sitting there right now with a desire (and plan) to write a book. I believe it is an act of destiny, and that this book within you that is waiting to come out could very well be the foundation for great things for yourself.

But sometimes before you can achieve great things, you must first see them.

So, let's take a journey into the reason why you are writing this book and, more specifically, the wider vision for your life and how this book serves to manifest that vision.

I once learned from a spiritual mentor that the four biggest questions that human beings ask are "Where did I come from?", "Where am I going?", "Who am I?" and "Why am I here?". These are incredibly pertinent here, as it is in the answers to these questions that we begin to see and imagine greater possibilities for our lives and ourselves.

When we comprehend the deeper meaning of our existence (a big topic, I know) and develop a sense of purpose within ourselves, we begin to dream for our future – or rather, tap into the dreams that are already present within us. We become ignited with a vision greater than our circumstances, and that vision becomes our driving force to tackle all our goals: goals like writing a book.

There's a famous proverb that states that *"Without vision, the people will perish."* This relates to the journey of becoming an author, as those people who can clearly picture the impact they wish to make on the world are undoubtedly the ones who go the furthest and achieve the greatest results with their books.

Their personal connection to their message, combined with their conviction in the power that message has in and for the lives of others, drives them to lead from the front, to market their book broadly, to show up to opportunities, to create speaking opportunities, to do book signings, and to take the power of being an author with both hands and run with it.

Their vision helps to tap into the confidence and courage they need to step out into the limelight and be *known*. It helps them to embrace themselves for who they are and love their human shadows, all so they can make the contribution to humanity that they dream of and know they can achieve. Put simply; it helps them to get past their fears and insecurities and shine brightly for the sake of igniting a spark within others.

Those authors who live and work with vision are typically also the ones who produce books that change people's futures. This is partly because their vision drove them to make sure the book reached the hands of the people for whom it was written, and partly because they see their book as a chance to help someone else live a more fulfilling life.

It's not just words on a page to them; it's a way to reach into the lives of more people. It's not just a business card; it's a method of empowering and inspiring more people to seize the day and accept all that life has in store for them. And it's not just a book for the sake of it; it's a book with a higher purpose to leave their legacy through helping as many people as possible. They see it as something to offer to the world, something to enhance their clients' and customers' lives, something to leave behind them when they die.

This is why it's so important to *see great things* for yourself: to see more, dream of more, and get clear on what that 'more' is. Because if you do, you will write a book that truly will take you to great places, and if you don't, you will miss out on the many rewards that come from the permanent increase in professional credibility and influence that writing a book with vision brings you.

In case no one has ever told you that you are capable of great things, here it is:

YOU ARE CAPABLE OF GREAT THINGS.

YES. You are. I know, sometimes you think you're ordinary. I know sometimes you compare yourself to the leaders of the industry you're in and think that you are in some way less than them – or that there is no room for you at the top. But here's the thing:

You were BORN for the top!

You were not born small; you may just play small. You were not born without potential; it is because of your potential that you were born. You were not born without reason; you were born with a specific end in mind. You were not born to suffer or to live an impoverished life; you were born to discover the infinite wealth within you and earn a fortune sharing that with the world.

Keep this in mind as you answer the following questions:

3: See great things for yourself

What is the higher purpose for my life?

For what important reason was I placed on the planet?

What kind of life could I live by being in service to the world?

And now, let's invite your book to the party:

What important message does this book allow me to communicate?

Once this book is published, where could I take it and where could it take me?

And,

How can I use this book to change the world?

Give yourself permission to find and own your strengths. Be courageous enough to put them in the spotlight, to share what you feel, to teach what you know, and to show people what it is that you can really do. Show them who really are. Let the world love you for who you are. Follow your bliss and it will take you to great places.

Writing a book is not a small act — it is a BIG one. So, have the book that you write be part of your mission and purpose in life. Use it as a tool to express who you are, teach what you know and change lives. And through that, invite your book to play a significant role in making all your dreams come true.

The world is waiting to hear your unique message.

4: Writing is a sacred practice, so treat it like one

> *"When you sell a man a book, you don't just sell him twelve ounces of paper and ink and glue: you sell him a whole new life."*
> **Christopher Morley**

Over my years of coaching people, I have witnessed people who'd previously said they weren't writers produce profound and inspiring books. I have seen people who have never written before channel tens of thousands of words onto the page (and have their life changed by doing it). And I've seen people who have dyslexia and dyspraxia push through their difficulties to become published authors.

And so, I believe to my core that a deeply transformational experience of writing is available to every human being, regardless of how well they think they write. However, what determines whether writing feels like a privilege or a drag when you sit down at your computer rests on your *attitude* and *approach* to it. AND, therefore, the power to transform your experience of writing into one that transforms *you* rests within you (and you only).

Do you dread the idea of sitting down and typing to produce your manuscript? Or do you look forward to it, knowing that every word you write closes the gap between you and your perfect reader?

For me, writing has been a sacred practice for more than twenty years. I wrote extensively as a child (mostly short stories about puppy dogs, kittens and budgerigars), however it was when I hit the emotionally-intense age of 14 that I began to use my writing as therapy instead of 'just' a creative outlet. I had been struggling to fit in at school and, not unlike many teenagers, I didn't feel my parents understood nor appreciated what I was feeling as I tried to find my place in the landscape of humanity.

I still remember the night that I began: the memory is as clear as day in my mind, even now. It was around 9:00pm one Friday and I'd had a rough week at school. I sat down in my family's computer room and opened a blank Word document on the computer. With only the glowing of the computer screen lighting up the room, I wrote a poem about

4: Writing is a sacred practice, so treat it like one

the tension and pain I felt inside me. I finally let it out... and I set myself free.

That was the moment my writing became a sacred practice. That was the moment I realized that this action of putting words on paper could be the saviour that I needed, and that, actually, I didn't necessarily need the people around me to know or like me: *I* needed to know and like me. My healing began and suddenly it didn't matter so much if I fit in or if people understood me, including my parents and peers.

In the year that followed, I wrote more than 170 poems, as well as several longer pieces of poetic prose. At the end of the year, I printed and bound forty copies of the book and gave them out to my teachers and friends at school. While some of my teachers were concerned about me (some of my writing expressed feelings of being lost and alone), several of my girlfriends thanked me for my writing, saying it helped them to find peace with their own problems.

I was fortunate to have experienced this at such a young age as it cemented in my mind that "When I write, I help and heal others." If you have followed me on social media, read any of my other published works, or spent any real length of time with me, then you will (hopefully) notice that this – my desire to touch and inspire people's lives in a meaningful way – is at the heart of everything that I do and have done.

I truly believe that just by sharing from the deepest parts of my life and myself, that I can stir power, confidence, courage and strength from within people. If I pour myself into my writings, this gives other people the permission they need to go after their dreams in life instead of putting themselves at the bottom of the pile.

So, here is a question for you:

How can bearing your heart on the page *not* be a sacred practice?

And,

How can passing on the knowledge you've acquired to change other people's lives *not* be a sacred act?

When you sit down to write, you make magic possible. You open yourself up to connect with and discover all that is within you. You come to heal all that is not healed within you, firm up your teachings, and consolidate your knowledge, all of which makes you a more influential individual: someone who other people turn to in a time of need or when they are seeking to learn a new skill.

Your words reach into the life of your reader. They encourage and inspire the reader to get through their challenges. They provide hope, strategies and answers to those who read them. They can even unlock a whole new lease on life and a vision for a greater future.

4: Writing is a sacred practice, so treat it like one

I don't believe in banging out a book for the sake of it, like too many self-published authors do today (and many book coaches encourage people to do). This is because I *know* to my core how transformational the process of writing is for both the author and the reader. I know that trying to dodge the deep thinking and feeling that is often involved in producing a literary masterpiece often produces a book no better than every other book already published on the topic. I know that a book written with *true* heart and genuine intention will always trump one that is full of unoriginal, repetitive content.

I once coached a client who took nearly thirteen years to write his book. "Whoa!" I hear you saying to yourself. And yes, I also hear you saying, "There's no way I want *my* book to take that long!" I understand – and I'm not sharing this to encourage you to spend the better part of a decade toiling away on your manuscript.

I share this simply to encourage you to take off any *unnecessary* time pressure that would rush you too quickly through the process of writing a book. Doing so will cost you quality, inspiration and yes, perfection, in your final work. (By the way, the client's book was extraordinary and neither my book reviewer nor I could put it down!)

You have a deep and infinite well of valuable insight and wisdom inside you. You have not just one but *many* books within you. As you approach your writing practice with a curiosity and humbleness for the gifts it can bring you, you will be rewarded as it begins to flow out of you. Your self-belief will increase as the words move from your heart and soul through your mind and out onto the page.

Honour the practice of writing by setting up a sacred space for yourself whenever you write. Choose where you will write: it could be a room in a house, a local café, a hotel room, or a week-long writing retreat. If you must, make a grand gesture to support your writing process (for example, blocking two weeks out of your calendar to produce your book). Find the ideal length of time to write that synchronises with your schedule and other Earthly obligations – such as children, business or clients. This might be one to two hours first thing in the morning, half of each day, one day a week, the weekends, the Christmas period. It's up to you!

Then, be sure to place boundaries around the time you have created for yourself to simply write. Spend time journaling about what you are grateful for before you begin to work on your manuscript. Use candles, clothing, and the right music to create the ambience for your noble work. Take regular breaks (every two hours) to eat, get fresh air, and gain further inspiration for your book. Engage with a writing coach and the support team around you to spur you on through the journey to becoming an author.

4: Writing is a sacred practice, so treat it like one

And then, *surrender* to the writing process.

Choose your starting point in the book and START!

Dive in. Explore your heart and mind. Find and meet yourself on the page. Relax and let the words flow out from within you. Share your world with the readers. And remember that you *will* be rewarded ten-fold – with beautiful words, deep insights, and personal breakthroughs – every time you enter your writing zone, treating it like the sacred practice it is.

5: Focus on the message and the words will come

"My aim is to put down on paper what I see and what I feel in the best and simplest way."
Ernest Hemingway

Writer's block is an experience that most aspiring authors dread. In fact, many of the people I have acted as a book midwife for over the years have expressed a sense of trepidation before beginning their book. They say, "What if my writing isn't good?" and "What if I get halfway through my book and don't know what to write next?"

Yep, the idea of sitting and staring at a blank page feeling empty or lost inside is terrifying. And yep, even I try to avoid it at all costs when I write my own manuscripts. It's a completely understandable reason to get a case of the quivers when you decide to follow through on your desire to become an author. You don't want to feel that you've failed along the way or that you're falling short of the vision you have about how your book can be (you know, the dream you hold inside your mind about the ultimate end outcome for your published work).

I have delivered extensive advice to those who experience this concern about their writing being inferior or running out of words and thus, not being able to finish their book. This advice has ranged from encouraging them to believe in themselves to being sure that they have set up the right environment and schedule to back them in bringing the project to fruition.

But the advice that always works wonders – and that I find is the most poignant for dispelling this worry – is:

When you focus on the MESSAGE, the WORDS will come.

If you spend all your allocated writing time fiddling with a sentence, swapping words around, deleting parts of it, and re-editing it, then I can guarantee that you are likely to have a painful experience in writing your book. This is a shame, as getting too stuck on the actual words you use to communicate your message to people will trip you up, cut off or prevent your writing flow, or double (or more) the time frame it takes you to complete your first rough manuscript.

5: Focus on the message and the words will come

But, when you focus on *what you want to say* and *what you can't wait to share with the reader*, you put your conscious mind to work on a far more important task: educating, empowering and inspiring people by getting the words onto the page. This conscious focus on the higher mission of your book – to better the lives of your readers in one or many ways – will help you to transcend the habit of being too picky. You'll cease deliberating over whether to use 'delicious' or 'divine' in a single sentence and slip into the writing zone where you fill thousands of words in the pages of your book in a single day.

Trust me when I say you don't have to be a grammar goddess or a punctuation prince to write a phenomenal book. Your primary job during the production of your manuscript is to WRITE, not to REVIEW, and certainly not to EDIT. It is only once you have written a majority of the content into the book manuscript that it becomes time to shift modes from writing to reviewing.

As for editing? That is a job you must *never* do yourself! You are simply too close to the project – emotionally, mentally and otherwise – and you are likely underqualified to perform the proper 'polish' of your book to prepare it for publishing. In fact, editing is considered the first formal step in the process of producing a book in print or for online registration as an eBook.

At the young age of 21, I created the first manuscript of Dr. John Demartini's book *Inspired Destiny: Living A Fulfilling & Purposeful Life* for Hay House. I began with a blank document and built the first manuscript for the book through 220 pages of transcript and interviews with Dr. Demartini.

During this time, Dr. Demartini said to me that, "Inspired writing requires less editing." My extensive personal experience has certainly reflected this. When you are in an inspired state of mind where the words simply *pour* out of you onto the page, your writing will become *better*. New ways to express and explain things will just 'happen' – as if by magic – and you may even find that you begin to *love* the book you are writing. It's not narcissistic to feel that way. In fact, I hope you experience it, as it brings me great joy when I suddenly find myself dancing at my desk after punching out a sentence that sounds epic when read aloud.

I believe so deeply in the power of open-hearted writing (inspired writing) that I often walk away from my laptop, go get inspired, remember *what I really want to say*, and then come back to it a few hours or days later when I feel I can't *wait* to write. I know that whatever I produce in that high intensity channelled state of mind is going to put whatever I would have written while trying to wade through sludge and force writing to happen to shame.

5: Focus on the message and the words will come

As a sidenote, it's worth saying that I also follow this practice of walking away to get reconnected or connected with the MESSAGE I want to share beyond just book writing. I apply it when I am producing sales copy for my business, marketing emails, content for my social media, and more. In the lead-up to writing this book, I was producing a piece of long copy – the sales letter for my life planning program. I had been working on it for several weeks, piecing bits together to try and make it whole.

When it came to the time block I had scheduled to finish the copy, I found myself physically exhausted. So, I went for a swim and got an early night. The next morning, after a solid eight-hour sleep and breakfast, I wrote a near-flawless 1800-word long invitation letter to participants in 90 minutes. I wrote it front-to-back without back-tracking and it required very little editing. I'd let go of the struggle I'd been having – even let go of my attachment to running the actual course – and boom! There it was: a beautiful and inspiring piece of sales copy that had my heart and my belief in a greater life for the people on the other end etched in every word. Mwah!

I would go as far as to say that words written in an inspired state of mind have ten times the power of those that felt like drawing blood out of a stone. This is why you must draw on your inspiration and what is *within* you in order to a) tap into writing flow, and b) be the author of a book that people can't put down. Yes, this also means working to make sure that you are *inspired* in your life so that you can write well and frequently. This is one of the many profound gifts the writing journey can offer you.

A client once asked me how I find my inspiration for my writing, and when I responded that I made sure my life was full of the things that inspire me so that the inspiration would "overflow" onto the page, I realized how becoming a writer had changed my life so dramatically. My search for the right words to share with the world had ended up inspiring *me* as I then had nothing *but* inspired stimulus around me: from great conversations to incredible people to travel and a business I loved.

Without knowing it, I had gone searching for the source of the words – the MESSAGES I believed were worth sharing with the world. My pursuit of my mission to inspire people with the written wisdom had not only enabled me to become a prolific author (eight books published by age 28, releasing two per year three years running) but to experience significant rewards on a personal level through the knowledge that I was and am receiving the best life has to offer.

So, if you're feeling stuck when you are writing your book – I'm picturing you sitting at your computer, head in hands, dreaming of going to play outside

5: Focus on the message and the words will come

instead of writing your book – I want you to try the following:

1. Lean back in your chair or step away from your computer screen for a moment.
2. Close your eyes and take a deep breath.
3. Bring your awareness into your heart and breathe again.
4. Now, remember why you are writing this book.
5. Focus on the subchapter or topic you are presently writing in the manuscript, *and*
6. Ask yourself, "What do I *really* want to say here?"

I have always found that when I do this, it reminds me to say what I want to say, instead of writing what I think I should write – or, indeed, what someone else has said before me. It helps me to tap into the *original* and *inspiring* perspective that I can share on that topic. And, it supports me by drawing my attention away from the outside world.

You wouldn't be writing this book if you didn't care. You wouldn't be writing this book if your story wasn't worth sharing. And you wouldn't be writing this book if you weren't moved from *within* to do so. So, write from YOUR heart and YOUR mind. Share from the life that YOU have lived, and the wisdom that has changed your life when you accumulated and applied it. Don't write what you think people will like or what you think will please them. Write what is true for YOU. Let your truth out.

That's where the best books come from and it's what will make your book best-seller worthy.

Changing your focus from the words on the page to the message you feel compelled to publish in a book under your name will open a torrent of words from within you. It is there and then that you will experience the *richness* inside yourself. You ARE brilliant, and you DO have something powerful to share with other people. And once you have finished writing the manuscript, you can (and should) hire an editor to help you in turning your rough-cut diamond into a bright and shiny finished product.

Remember this as you write, and relax in the knowledge that you are *not in this alone!* 'All' you have to do is stay committed and devoted to putting the message you believe in – the message of your life – into the book. And then, find the right people to support you in finishing the job to transform that Word document into a book people can't wait to read.

Focus on the message... and the words will come!

6: Unite your life with your book and your book with your life

"Love is easy, and I love writing. You can't resist love. You get an idea, someone says something, and you're in love."

Ray Bradbury

I once said to a client that the best confirmation that you are writing the so-called 'right' book for you is when the walls between the book and your life begin to melt away.

Suddenly, it doesn't feel like the book project is a separate job to complete: it feels like the words on the page are an extension of you. It suddenly feels like inspiration for content is everywhere in the world around you: in conversations, on billboards and signs, in newspaper headlines, magazine articles, and even in your dreams at night-time. It suddenly seems like every time you turn around, there is another idea offering itself to you.

This is when your book and your life become ONE – and yes, it's delicious!

This is undoubtedly one of the greatest experiences of joy a writer can have, especially as they dive into their first book. I'm sending a prayer to the heavens that you are blessed to experience this for yourself, and not just once, but many, many, many times over your lifetime: because it is *transformational!* Magical. Enlightening. Heart-opening.

Writing that book – the 'right' one – seems to put everything else in your life into its proper perspective. Problems that you have or had don't seem to matter as much as you thought they did (and sometimes investing time into writing can bring you much-needed answers or creative solutions). Uninspiring friendships and relationships start to fade away into the background and then out of your life completely. Even self-doubt – the internal voice that doesn't play big like the rest of you wants to – seems to take a backseat and allows the greater version of you to steer the car.

Life begins to feel different as each day becomes an adventure into the vortex of your book.

6: Unite your life with your book and your book with your life

You can walk down the street and find yourself spontaneously inspired, leading you to grab the flat surface closest to you – a napkin, receipt, your T-shirt – to scribble down the all-important words that will later join the others to form your book manuscript. You can often find yourself saying, "Hang on a moment, I just need to write something down," to the person you are mid-conversation with because something they said has triggered a *genius* thought that's going to make your book that much sexier!

The inspiration for your book is all around you because you're tuned in to *why* what you are writing is so important and you feel so lucky to have been chosen as the one to make the book manifest in the world. (I believe that becoming and being an author is a privileged position to hold, one that is perhaps undervalued or not used as wisely as it could be.)

I love to give myself to my book writing process.

It might sound crazy, but writing brings out the very best in me. Perhaps this is because I work hard to bring the best out of myself for my books, as that is all I care about offering to people and the page. (I do wonder what the point of a career in writing would be if I didn't make that objective my priority?)

And so, when that devotion to writing is coupled with the presence of a book I can't wait to write and a message I can't wait to share (like the one I'm sharing with you right now), it transforms my state of mind. The fact that I feel the book is a book about my life – even if the topic might seem disconnected or separate on a logical level, perhaps sales and speaking in business, for example – assists me to *tap into* the 'write' state of mind.

I become IGNITED with the force of expression from within… and so will you!

When your book closely reflects what you believe in, you will find it hard to walk away from your computer, even if you are busting to go to the bathroom. You may even begin to lightly dread anything that takes you away from the book – including meal times! – simply because you are so inspired by the manuscript you are producing, and you experience such a high level of joy while working on it.

You might be sitting there right now wondering what you can do to unite your life with your book. And my answer to that?

Write the book that is inside your *HEART*.

Write the book that you *can't wait* to share with people.

And,

Write the book that makes you come alive!

That is where the magic is. That is where time stands still, and you feel connected to all that is and the

6: Unite your life with your book and your book with your life

power of your message. It is where your journey as a human being and the journey of your reader meld and become one; where you feel that you *are* your reader and that you are speaking to their soul through your words. That is where you will become interested in the activity of writing (even if you disliked it before) – because you are so deeply interested in the content that you're putting on the page. And that is where you will probably find yourself writing a book that you would honestly buy yourself if you saw it on a shelf with another person's name on it.

A book in which the topic and core message are based on what *actually* matters to you will be the one that gives *you* the sensation that there is no separation between you and the book you are writing. Every day of your life will become an opportunity to express what you believe in on paper in a way that helps other people.

You can also choose to deepen your connection to your current book by asking yourself:

Why do I care so much about writing this book?

You can draw the inspiration that you need from your own life to write it, if you choose to. It is possible that you are yet to recognise just how *rich* a source of content your life is and can be. If that is true, then I certainly encourage you to begin reflecting on the world within you more deeply! You might be surprised by what you find.

Inspiration truly is everywhere once you begin to view the world through the lens of a book you love. With the 'right' book in mind, even the slightest expression on someone's face or a titbit of a stranger's conversation can feel like an invitation to write.

I hope that you keep persisting with your writing journey until *YOUR* book and life become *ONE* and the words fall out of you onto the page.

7: Writing your book will change your life

"Writing is one of the few professions where you can psychoanalyse yourself, get rid of hostilities and frustrations in public, and get paid for it."

Octavia Butler

I have long believed that book writing is really a self-development program in disguise. Over the past decade, I have watched people discover new visions, find new confidence, and dream bigger because they decided to pursue their dream of becoming an author. I have also watched people finally put the past to rest (where it belongs) and turn their childhood adversities into stepping stones or launch pads for the future. And I have seen people figure out who they *really* are after producing a 60,000-word manuscript.

This phenomenon – of writing being such a transformational experience for the author – is one of the biggest sources of my inspiration as a prolific writer. I know that I become greater and my life becomes greater every time I write a book. I wouldn't be surprised if you get bitten by the writing bug and feel so ignited after writing your book that you find yourself spontaneously determined to publish several more. You too might just become hooked on the thrill of unleashing your potential by writing.

Having said this, writing your book might be one of the toughest goals to which you can set your mind. Putting your thoughts and grand ideas on paper might challenge every truth you've ever believed. Teaching what you know might take your existing content to an entirely new level. Sharing what is inside you might challenge you to let your walls down and accept that you ARE worthy of love, no matter what you have done or not done. And I'm not going to lie to you: sharing your life story with the higher intention of giving hope to those who are struggling with adversity might kick your butt at times.

But, I can promise you that no matter how intense the grace or the struggle you experience on the journey of becoming an author, it *will* change your life. That is a guarantee.

When I facilitate writing retreats, I absolutely cherish the moments when I can see the lives of the writers

7: Writing your book will change your life

change with each passing day. The participants often start the journey feeling excited about their book idea. Then they run into some form of trepidation and doubt, whether that is about whether people will read it, whether they are a 'good' writer, or whether they are courageous enough to write the story they intuitively know will help and heal those who read it.

As they are supported and support themselves through the process of writing, the trepidation turns back into excitement as they drop into the zone and experience the joy that often comes with FINALLY letting out what is within them. The journey continues, and, along the way, they free themselves from self-doubt, realise they know more than they think they know, comprehend the *true* value of their information, and find their feet as the leader, coach, consultant, speaker or advisor they wish to be.

The process of writing the book builds their confidence and – word by word – compounds that which they hold dear. The extensive internal reflection often required to write a book (at least a decent one) consolidates what they believe to be true. And they discover what I believe in my heart of hearts is the truth: that every human being is *extraordinary*.

It's not necessarily a journey for the faint-hearted, but those who summon the courage to face, find and express themselves on the page are rewarded greatly, in more ways than one.

One of my clients left her husband while writing her book. "How did that happen? It's *just* a book", you might wonder. Well, put simply, she was more than halfway through writing her book, which focused on empowering people to create a more enriching, empowered and fulfilling life, when she experienced the life-transforming epiphany that the person she was writing the book for was her husband.

It then occurred to her that she had been 'carrying', for want of a better word, him in his life. She had been trying, unconsciously and consciously, to invite and support him to lift his game: because she knew what was on offer if he invested in his own personal growth.

Naturally, this was a *huge* discovery for her. Life changing? DEFINITELY. It was a discovery that led her to decide she was ready for a new partner – or, at least, that she no longer felt it was her job to 'fix' or help her then-husband. When I talked about this breakthrough with her, she simply expressed that she couldn't keep living this way if she was going to walk her talk in the world. I stood back and watched as she courageously ended the marriage and reclaimed what you might refer to as her true identity by changing her last name back to her maiden name…. just in time to publish the book!

While this story is certainly on the intense end of the spectrum (perhaps I ought to include a disclaimer in my writing coaching and retreats that warns people of possible life-altering revelations that may occur!), it is an appropriate example of just how significantly your life can change as you write.

See, it's not *'just'* writing; it's a chance to shed old layers and make a quantum leap in your life. It's not just writing; it's an opportunity to consolidate your central message and teachings for a keynote presentation. It's not just writing; it's a space for you to connect with and discover the topics that you are deeply inspired by (that I would recommend making a career or business out of!).

So, what does this mean for your writing journey?

Well, first, it means making a commitment to yourself that you will not settle for an average book or a mediocre title; that you will not sell yourself short in this book. Bookstores around the world *only* stock books that have outstanding covers, that sell well, or that were recommended to them time and time again. So, it pays to devote yourself to writing an extraordinary book (that's also what will change your life the most).

It also means being patient enough with the process of writing to check, reflect on and confirm that what you are about to publish IS what you want to say and what you believe in – and that you are comfortable with it going down in ISBN history. And it also means taking the time to carefully align your book with your business and vision, so that when the book is published, it helps you to establish the foundation for your future.

Then, it is about deciding that you will do what it takes to be present while you write every word of the manuscript. It is only in that space – where you are mentally 'logged in' to what you are writing and why you are writing it – that the book will begin to give more back to you than you give to it.

I'm a strong advocate for the wisdom that, if a book doesn't change you while you're writing it then it may not be a book worth reading. I also believe that the books where the author became a new version of themselves through writing it, are usually the books that go viral once published, because the transformation of the author is written on the pages of the book.

Prepare for the greatest ride of your life because as your book changes you, it will, in turn, change your life.

8: Grow into your content

"The worst enemy to creativity is self-doubt."
Sylvia Plath

It's a common misconception of new authors that you will know every single word of your book before you write it. In fact, that's a flat-out myth that I feel a responsibility to bust for you just in case it is the reason you haven't yet taken the plunge to start your book!

You may begin writing your manuscript with a plan in mind, but I have no doubt that as you continue to venture down the yellow brick road dedicated to your mission to become an author, you will discover new interesting things to say. You will find yourself writing about topics that you didn't even *know* that you are a genius in.

You're likely to fall in love with your content more deeply than before, tap into new ideas for your teachings, and take your message to a new level. You're also likely to, at some point, have an epiphany that is not just central to but *vital* to the book. Honouring this may require shifting or refining one or many parts of the book – from your subtitles and chapter headings, to the order of your chapters.

It's NORMAL for your book to evolve and morph as you write it. And, more importantly – perhaps *most* importantly – you might *never* feel ready to write your book. The reason for this is that you *will grow into your content* as you write it!

Not one of the eight-plus books I've written turned out the way I originally planned (the control freak in me has issues with this sometimes but my higher self knows better!). In fact, some of them ended up as a radically different but *much* improved version of my original idea. And the only way I could reach that point? By trusting the process, holding the end vision of the book firmly in my mind as I wrote, and *allowing* myself to go on a journey of discovery as I tapped out the words of my manuscript with my fingertips.

You could liken it to the tale of a warrior who ventures out into a new part of the world to quickly find that he is supported with signs, prompts and messages from the land and heavens as he makes his way into new territory. While he may have felt nervous

8: Grow into your content

at the beginning, despite being armed with a map of the land, he soon realises that this journey isn't as frightening as it may have felt at first. In fact, he is more determined than ever to make the journey when he discovers the many wonders that await him along the path and at the final destination.

You are not alone in the writing process and, if you are writing a book that lights you up from within, then you WILL be guided as you follow the twists and turns of your journey, with the end vision for your book and the bigger vision for your life as your guiding star.

As you write your story, you will connect with the message you *live* to share with the world – and not just through your book, but your brand, business, programs, products, philanthropic projects and services. As you teach your content, you'll further develop your coaching process or model and end up adding 5,000 more words. Or, you will get halfway through writing what you thought was a generic how-to business book and wake up in the middle of the night overcome with a sudden realisation. You're not just helping people grow a business, you are, in actual fact, writing a book about your *life* because business is so important to you.

You will FIND what you want to say as you embark on the journey of writing what you already know you want to say. You will begin with the initial spark for your book (the idea), plan the topics you want to include in the book, and then immerse yourself in the journey of writing, ready and willing to *grow* into *YOUR* content.

Imagine if writing this book could help you to grow your confidence.

Imagine if writing this book could help you make peace with the past.

And imagine if writing this book could help you gain clarity on who you are and

THAT is what growing into your content is about: it's about *growing YOU*.

I have often said that there is a book inside every business. And so, if you are intending to use your book to start a business or perhaps to launch a new service, mastermind or product to a new target market or your existing customers, then writing a book may be one of the most powerful things that you do, as it allows you to *clarify* your content as you write.

Although I wouldn't necessarily recommend writing a book *just* to clarify your message (this may leave you with an unstructured mess), even the process of mapping out your plan for the book can be exponentially powerful in helping people to piece together their unique process, model or message. It can start that all-important journey toward realising that you DO have content worth sharing in a book – and knowing what that content is.

8: Grow into your content

I've seen it many times with my one-on-one coaching clients. The light just suddenly goes on during the planning phase. Then, as they begin to get their feet wet with the actual writing of the book, they are often amazed at the treasures they find: even if they're only writing the introduction of the book!

So, remember as you move forwards that where you start is not where you will end, and that you will grow in ways you can't predict or imagine as you sit there reading this right now.

All that is left for you to do is *take the journey!*

9: Your readers can feel you

"When you speak, your words echo across the room. When you write, your words echo across the ages."
Bud Gardner

What I am about to share is arguably the most powerful wisdom I can teach you if you want to master the art of changing lives with your words (so sit up and read on!).

If you begin to apply this wisdom to your writing process – whether that is a book, blog, emails, proposal, sales letter, or article – then you will tap into a whole new realm of quality with your writing, not to mention significantly increase the chances of receiving rave reviews about your book once it is published. I learned this wisdom nearly a decade ago and it has stayed with me ever since. It is the one insight that I keep close to my side every single time I write, without fail. That's how powerful it is.

Here it is:

Your readers can feel you.

This might sound creepy upon first impact (Big Brother is watching you!) but let me explain so it makes sense. See, I believe that words have vibrations and that they also carry the vibrations of the person communicating them.

When you write, the vibration you are 'in' becomes transferred onto the page: like an imprint or a snapshot of how you 'were' in that moment. The vibration then travels with the words wherever they go and, without you having to do *anything*, it touches the person reading it.

If the author felt pensive or sad while writing the book, you will feel that when you read what they've written. If the author felt powerful and inspired while producing the content, you will feel that too. And if the author poured their heart out while telling a story about how they hit rock bottom and bounced back again, it is highly likely that you will feel every part of their rollercoaster journey as they detail it on the page.

Have you ever seen someone walk into a room and their presence lights it up? And, on the flip side,

9: Your readers can feel you

have you ever experienced someone walking into a room and suddenly the entire room feels unsettled? That's what I'm talking about here. We carry an energy around us (like an aura) wherever we go and, depending on the state of mind we are in, we influence those who cross our paths. Embodying this wisdom is about realising that this principle also applies to the process and art of writing a book.

This applies regardless of how long the time is between the moment the words were written and the moment the words were read. Think about all the writing you have read that was produced days, weeks, months, years or decades before your eyes met the page. The vibration and presence of the author – and their connection to and affinity for their message or teachings – *still* touches you even though they aren't sitting right there with you.

The profound philosophical writings of Ralph Waldo Emerson, the poem famously quoted from Marianne Williamson about it being our light (not our darkness) that we are most afraid of, and the historically famous speech by Martin Luther King Jr titled *I Have A Dream* are perfect examples of how the presence of an author rippled through time – and they can still be felt today. I am sure you can think of a long line of your favourite writings: writings that you still refer to in times when you need inspiration, hope or simply the warmth that they provided (I have many of my favourite pieces on a wall in my home).

Their messages transcended the time and space in which they was first expressed to touch the lives of millions of people across the face of the Earth. Their words carried across the ages, capturing the hearts of the people whose souls these authors, writers and inspirational messengers intended to reach out and touch.

You might be wondering how to activate this writing superpower so that every time you write, your words also ripple out and travel to greater places. And really? It's quite simple:

1. **Choose the energy you want your writing to have,** and

2. **Embody that energy *before* you write.**

Do you want your readers to feel powerful after reading the book? If so, feel powerful as you are writing. Do you want your readers to heal deeply as they journey through your words? If so, carry and intend a healing energy as you tap out the content for your book. Applying this practice in your writing practice *will* push you to become further aligned with your message and both expand and deepen the impact you have on your target reader.

I was mentoring a client to write her book several years ago. It was a self-help book that empowered

9: Your readers can feel you

people to make their life their choice (a powerful message, when embodied). I had been coaching the client for several months and her manuscript was coming along nicely. I would perform regular reviews of her content between coaching sessions.

One day, I was reading the content she had recently added to the manuscript when I reached a point in the book where I began feeling agitated. The feeling seemed to come out of nowhere. In fact, I almost felt angry! Having no external stimulus other than her book at the time, I remembered that the energy we write with *does* transfer onto the page for the reader to feel.

So, on our next coaching call, I asked her to reflect on how she had been feeling while writing that subchapter in the book. Guess what her response was? You got it: "I was feeling angry! I had just received a call from someone who had pushed my buttons because a problem we've been trying to solve isn't working out." Then she paused for a moment and asked me *why* I asked her that.

I smiled on the inside, explained to her that it was because I had felt angry while reading that part of her book, and then gently suggested to her that she rewrite that section when in the 'write' state of mind. Thankfully, she agreed. It goes without saying that the new words she replaced the old content with were *much* better and a joy to read!

In a nutshell, this wisdom is about the power of open-hearted writing.

It is about the state of mind that you are in when you bring words to the page.

And, it is about how you show up in the writing process.

YOU have the most important role in bringing your book to life. You are the visionary who decided to pursue the book idea and invest yourself into writing it. You are the one with the content, message, story and concepts in your mind who wants to share it with the world. And so, it *matters* how you feel when you sit down to write.

It *matters* how you look after yourself so that you are sharp, not sluggish, during pre-set focused writing time. It *matters* that you bring enthusiasm, determination, persistence and inspiration to the forefront while writing (who wants to read a book that the author hated writing?). And it *matters* that you do everything possible to make your book-writing journey an inspirational and transformational one.

Every action you take while producing your manuscript will be reflected in the many pages of your published book, so choose your actions wisely. Each thought and feeling will come together to form a written and printed representation of who you are. And you know what? *People* will make up

9: Your readers can feel you

their mind how they feel and what they think about based on the book you write.

I certainly don't say that to make you paranoid or overly nervous to the point where it interferes with your writing process. I DO say it because I want you to know that the power to write a book that is loved by the readers – one they feel they've been waiting to read – is within you! You have the power to choose how you want your book to sound, look and feel, and how you want your readers to feel as they read your finished product.

I have always believed that my best writing occurs when I hit a point where I am *so* intimately connected with a message that I push everything else aside to get it out onto the page – to make sure that I capture it before it slips away from me. I write with pace, fuelled by a deep determination to say what I believe is important for other people to know, hear or feel. When I write like that for people, my social media posts receive the greatest number of reactions and shares, my blogs get circulated, and my books generate a flow of inbox messages and emails in which people thank me for what I wrote because it uplifted their day or even saved their life. Yes, I have had people say that to me: an experience I almost don't have words for.

Because I care so strongly about producing this type of words – the world-touching, life-changing kind – I invest a significant amount of time into aligning my state of mind with the message I *really* wish to get across in my book. I ensure that I *feel* how I want the reader to feel before my fingertips connect with the keyboard.

How do I do this?

I write down as many things I am thankful for as possible before I open my Word document.

I work with and draw on insight from my own mentors to stimulate my mind.

I remember and remind myself of my bigger vision and the bigger vision for my book.

I ensure I am in the 'write' environment; one that inspires my mind from the outside-in.

I organise my day and life so that I can work for several hours at a time undisturbed – typically a minimum of two, in case you were wondering.

I stop to think about the reader and all the challenges they're facing in their life (the ones I can help them to resolve).

And, I continually work on resolving my personal challenges and solving my problems: to make me a 'better' writer.

That's how much I care about producing great writing. I care about it so much that I would almost go as far as to say that the purpose of the extensive

9: Your readers can feel you

self-development work that I complete daily is so that I *can* impact other people's lives with my words. I know that I really can't hide behind the words on the page: in fact, quite the opposite.

And so, I embrace it as the grand and powerful opportunity that it is: the chance to reach into the life of another human being and help them to do something they have been struggling to do on their own.

Take a leaf out of my book and choose to do the same.

Choose to empower your readers.

Choose to fill them with hope.

Choose to teach and prepare them for success.

And choose to, through whichever book you write, inspire them!

10: Bear your soul on the page

"Every secret of a writer's soul, every experience of his life, every quality of his mind, is written large in his works."
Virginia Woolf

It's a common occurrence in my profession that people approach me and tell me that they want to write their personal story. It fact, it happens so frequently that I sometimes wonder if I have a sign stamped on my forehead that reads: "Want to publish your personal story? I can help!" Every week or so, someone will send me a message or come up to me at a networking event and ask if I can coach them to write their life story of overcoming adversity, so they can use the book to inspire hope in people.

It has been a great privilege to stand by and support hundreds of people over the years as they pour their heart out onto the page, telling the tale of their darkest moments and how they became who they are today.

I have heard and read many stories that would make you shake your head wondering how the person managed to come out the other side in one piece, stories that show the true strength of the human spirit once we become determined not to let life get the better of us, and stories that leave you feeling to your core that everything and anything you dream of truly is possible.

I have received great inspiration from these stories and, even more so, the people who had the courage to bear their soul on the page for the 'greater good' of humanity. These are the people who cared enough to reveal their darkest times to lead others into the light.

They are the ones who bravely exposed themselves and their past adversities to provide the strength that other people need to defeat their obstacles. And they are the individuals who knew that, by sharing their story, they could give another person the belief that a total life transformation is possible.

A client once asked me how I manage to find the courage to be so vulnerable in the way I share my life with people I have only just met. She knew that

10: Bear your soul on the page

I had spent more than ten years revealing my story of overcoming depression at age 19 (a rock-bottom moment where I wanted to take my life by running my car into a concrete wall). I had voiced this on stages with audiences from Australia and around the world, had published it in several books, not just including my own, and shared it in a long line of podcasts and interview series.

As I sat and reflected on the answer to her question (my answer is coming, don't worry!), I suddenly realised that the courage to truly bear one's soul to the world doesn't necessarily come easily for everyone.

It occurred to me that sometimes the hardest thing *to* do is to open up and disclose your history, how you felt about it at the time, and what you learned from it personally to another human being. And it reminded me that when I first started to share my story and speak from stage and on video, I too was terrified to show up and expose my story.

Perhaps you are one of these people: someone who has lived a thousand lives in one and whose life story could, quite frankly, be turned into a Hollywood movie but who is terrified to even start the process of writing a book. If this is true, then you might be questioning how much to share in your book or wondering how you are going to find the courage it will require to write a story that is so personal to you.

And if so, this message here is for *you* – and here's what it is:

Always remember that the reward of watching someone else's life changing because you had the courage to share your story is greater than the pain you will experience in sharing it.

Whenever I am about to stand on stage or sit down to write my personal story, I take my attention off myself and place it on the audience or reader. I focus on the fact that I have a group of individuals in front of me who might be feeling lost and for whom my story might provide insight. And I make it my mission to share my story as an *offering* to them on the off chance that it helps them to make a breakthrough in their own life.

Take this approach when it comes to you sharing your own story. View your story as an invitation the reader: an invitation for them to move past whatever struggle they face (a struggle that you have likely been through and came out the other side of for yourself) and achieve, be, have and experience more in their life in one or more areas. I can promise you that if you do this – if you share openly from your own experiences, your trials, your tribulations, your wins and your breakthroughs – you will create warmer relationships with your readers than if you hold it all in, trying to appear cool, calm and collected one hundred percent of the time.

10: Bear your soul on the page

Draw on the courage within you by remembering that if you are bold enough to tell people about the challenges you faced and describe them in detail while also teaching them how you managed to get past your obstacles — be they internal or external — then you invite people to share their story with you in return. And in the space that opens up due to *you* opening up? Well, in that space, great healing, miracles, and a new lease on life become possible.

I also know that harnessing this courage to bear your soul on paper can apply to sharing just *one* story from your life, not the whole gig. I've noticed this reaps many therapeutic and mental-emotional benefits, as the person comprehends and reflects on their life through writing about it.

I encountered a moment while writing the book that will be published after *this* book (remember, I momentarily stopped writing another manuscript to birth this one!). I was detailing a business and financial model for the reader in one of my chapters. While I was writing that subchapter in the book, I suddenly found myself compelled to reveal an extremely personal story that detailed one of the toughest challenges I had faced in my own business trajectory. I couldn't help myself: my fingers just kept on typing and the story just kept on flowing out of me.

The story felt so raw to write about that I thought about taking it out of the book, mostly because it was still a fresh experience in my life. But then I remembered that the purpose of sharing the story was to prepare the reader to take proper care of their financials, so they didn't risk losing their love of what they do because of financial challenges.

I remembered that someone else might take the time to learn about managing money wisely in their company if they knew what might happen if they don't. And, I remembered that me sharing this story might be the difference between someone giving up on their mission in life and suppressing the dreams within them, or doing whatever it takes to go the distance and thrive both professionally and financially.

You've already guessed what I decided to do: I decided to leave the story in the book. I chose to be strong enough and to love myself enough to tell them the truth, for the sake of their own fulfilment and future. I knew that if I *did* share it, then the reader would feel just *how* much I care about them creating a life they love – and they would certainly never question whether or not I am personally invested in the work that I do in the world.

I get it: you might be afraid that people will judge you, see you as less professional, label you unfairly, or stay away from you after they hear your story. BUT, it is important to trust that the right people will resonate with the journey you share. I have always found this

10: Bear your soul on the page

to be true, for myself and also for my clients who have published some or all of their story in a book.

They will be the ones who approach you for further help or advice. They will be the ones who want to spend more time with you. And they will be the ones who want to know how you did what you did. They might even become your raving fans that stay with you for the length of your career as an author, speaker, consultant, coach, entrepreneur, media profile, leader – you name it.

So, believe in the notion that if you courageously reveal all as you write your story, that the perfect clients – clients who almost feel like family to you – will read your book and hang on to every word you write. And remember that, at the end of the day, we are all in this together as one big human family.

11: You have an infinite well of content within you

"You don't write because you have to say something, you write because you have something to say."
F. Scott Fitzgerald

One of the greatest fears authors have about publishing a book is that someone, somewhere, will call them a fraud. It has surprised me how frequently I hear these words come out of a budding writer's mouth:

"What if someone calls me a hypocrite?"

Or

"What if people say I'm not qualified to write about this?"

They are afraid that by putting out a book exposing their innermost thoughts, personal story and feelings, that they will be subject to extensive criticism. They think their readers will focus on picking them apart piece-by-piece as they read through each chapter of their content. And, in some cases, they get what I refer to as 'page fright', which makes them want to crawl under the covers of their bed and avoid the spotlight completely.

Has this happened to authors in the past where they were challenged by the audience? I'm sure of it. Have books been written that stir up controversy and ruffle fears by questioning the norm? Absolutely. Are there authors who have been subject to what Australians typically refer to as 'tall poppy syndrome'? No doubt. Is the fear of this becoming a reality once your book hits print debilitating? Yes!

A fear like this can easily stop you in your tracks; it can cause you to start doubting yourself and question why you are writing your book. This is a real problem for the single reason that it will block your *original message* from coming out, thus delaying the impact that this message could and would have on the readers who are searching for the answers you have inside you.

I want to address this right here, right now, so that you can get on with the extremely important job of writing a book that could potentially help thousands of people.

The best way I know of to silence this voice of fear (and doubt in oneself, I might add) is to *write from what you know!*

11: You have an infinite well of content within you

To do this, you must first recognise that you have an *infinite* well of content within you that you can draw on when bringing your manuscript to fruition. You know far more than you think you know and it is highly likely that you do have a profound series of teachings that would, when shared with and taught to others, be incredibly valuable. In fact, I am sure that your personal experiences contain a wealth of information and wisdom in and of themselves – and that's without adding your professional qualifications into the mix.

It's just that most people – and certainly most of the authors who I have worked with – don't recognise this all-important truth. They kind of brush off the idea that they could be or are intelligent or knowledgeable; a genius in their field, even. They look to the leaders and top-notch presenters or influencers from their industry and instantly minimise themselves. They write themselves off or bench themselves before the game has even begun!

Take a moment right now to list out the top 10 topics that you *know* things about on the lines below; information that you could share with people:

1. _____
2. _____
3. _____
4. _____

5. _____
6. _____
7. _____
8. _____
9. _____
10. _____

Got it? Great! This initial acknowledgement of *what you know* – or sense that you have to offer – might be all you need to give yourself permission to write the epic book waiting inside you.

Then, as you are writing your actual book, I want you to write from what you know. Why? Because if you do this, then you will a) become unshakeable when your book is published, and b) build a *much* stronger foundation for yourself in business. This includes earning the respect of people who'll sense you've written what you know, not what *you* thought you should know.

In my career as an author and professional speaker, I have occasionally become aware of the fact that I don't have a University degree. I dropped out six months in to follow my heart into the world of personal transformation. I have occasionally encountered questions from people about what my qualifications are and what I studied in my degree. And yes, I often get asked how old I am. Apparently, I have a young

11: You have an infinite well of content within you

face, which doesn't always help me to build my case around looking or feeling credible – especially when added to the fact that I *am* young!

My one foolproof strategy for handling this is to *stick to what I know* and to write about that in the most engaging and inspiring way I can. I don't try to make up content or publish concepts in my book or preach a message unless and until I am certain of them. I want my books to be full of what I deeply believe and feel, not what I think I should say. I also want to publish works that stand the test of time and that capture my heart and soul on paper, rather than banging out a text that is relevant for one day and gone the next (a one-launch-wonder).

This strategy works for me – and it works every time. It also works for the authors I coach. When they run into the question of "Oh, but who am I to write about this?" I encourage them to sit for a moment and think about what it is that they *truly* wish to express or say on this topic.

I guide their attention away from the possible naysayers and back into their inner world, which is abundant with truths that are ready and ripe for the picking. And I remind them that certainty as an author comes from writing what you know rather than trying to conjure up fancy words on the page. I tell them to avoid writing about topics that they couldn't back up in real-life if questioned (for example, teaching a wealth-building strategy when they are broke personally).

So, write what you feel is true. Write what you know and feel is true.

The best check of whether you are comfortable with your content is to imagine yourself being interviewed about it on national TV. Would you feel comfortable saying what you write? Would you be able to handle the interviewer pressing you about your story or topics?

If you're not convinced that what you are writing about is truly your gospel – or if it truly is the best advice for the reader – then you have three options:

a) Delete the content completely and rewrite it from what you know,

b) Edit and/or adjust what you've written so it *does* feel right, or

c) Wait for yourself to 'grow into' the content you have written.

In the first option, you are making an executive decision to remove the content you don't feel confident about and write it fresh. This means cutting and pasting that part of your book into a separate Word document and coming back to the book manuscript to, yes, start that part again.

There is no loss in doing this. It's likely to be only small segments of your book, and remember: there

11: You have an infinite well of content within you

is an infinite well of content within you! I would be inclined to view it as a forward step instead of a backwards one, as the new content you write from what you absolutely know to be true will be worth its weight in gold (not to mention how much better you will feel about releasing the book).

I took this path during the writing of my third book, *The Unlikely Entrepreneur*. During the review stage of the book (between writing and editing), I found myself getting stuck every time I reached a specific point in the manuscript. I tried to review it several times – walking away from it each time and attempting to come back to it with a fresh mind – before I decided to talk it out with a team member.

As I did, I realised that I had written content that, really, wasn't mine: it was just something I had heard someone else say. And, when I was honest with myself, I was bored by it! In other words, it wasn't what I truly wanted to say about that topic.

I promptly deleted those three paragraphs of fluff from my book and replaced them with a fresh and sexy piece that I loved. Hey presto! It worked. I then flowed through the reviewing process without so much as a tiny bump in the road.

In the second option, you simply sit with what you have written – the part you are unsure about or that you think someone might question you on – and you adjust it until it sits right with you on every level. For example, if you've told them that the method you teach in your book is the *only* way to cure depression (which isn't true – and even I would question you on this!) then you might alter this to communicate the primary benefit of your method instead, e.g. a supported healing approach to aid with depression recovery.

Or perhaps you have claimed yourself to be the number one expert on a topic (number one according to who?). Phrases like this often open an author up to criticism. Be careful to prescribe only what you are certified to prescribe and to make it clear to the reader that you are writing from what *you* feel and *your* personal experiences. I find that when I write books as an offering to the reader – in case something that I've done for myself could work for them – my books are better received than if I had approached them with arrogance like a self-proclaimed guru trying to prove how good I am.

If you write from the wisdom already inside you, there will be no need for you to exaggerate what you put down on paper. You won't need to big-note yourself to lure people into doing business with you (which readers can see through, by the way). If you write authentically, drawing on the infinite well of content within you and from the richness of your own experiences, writing what you believe and feel in the

11: You have an infinite well of content within you

most accurate way possible, people will be naturally drawn to you. Your perfect clients will be magnetised towards you.

The third option you have when you smell a rat in your own book is to wait until you grow into the content you wish to teach. Let's say you are writing a book on business and it captures the main principles you have learned in your years of business. Perhaps you are comfortable with eighty percent of the content you have included in the book but there are some topics you want to include that you don't feel confident writing about yet. Maybe you haven't achieved the results in your business that would provide examples of what you're teaching.

In this scenario, you might simply choose to wait for a series of months and give yourself a longer time frame to accomplish a goal before you attempt the writing of the missing content. Alternatively, you could patiently wait until you feel ready to write about it by preparing yourself and taking some time to decide how you want to say it.

This will give you the time that you need to 'step into' the content if you do have the credibility to write about it and are simply lacking the confidence to do so. Or, it will provide you with the space required to heal up any part of you that doesn't believe you are worthy of success post-publish. Sometimes, the resistance we feel to writing and publishing our brilliance has to do with psychology and not our level of achievement. I've been there myself many times.

If you feel stuck for ideas about what to write or you feel the pressure of perfectionism and "I need more qualifications" closing in on you, try the following to get yourself back in flow and writing from what you know:

- Think back to an experience you had and what you learned from it,
- Deconstruct how you did something to teach someone else, or
- Share wisdom, a story or a message you know can help someone.

An entire body of work can be built out of what you know: you just need to believe that it is true and it will emerge from your very core. You have enough knowledge within you to fill a library, you just need to connect with the topics you can't wait to write about. You have wisdom deep enough that it could heal or save someone from the toughest situation in which they've ever found themselves.

You have an infinite well of content within you just waiting to come out.

12: Write for your readers

> *"The power of a book lies in its power to turn a solitary act into a shared vision."*
> **Laura Bush**

Becoming an author provides you with one of the most powerful forms of communication.

It enables you to document your knowledge, wisdom and story on paper. Then, it enables that knowledge, wisdom and story to travel through space (in the form of a book) and time (in the sense that your masterpiece won't go out of date) and land in the life of another human being. And, it allows the reader to go on a journey through the knowledge, wisdom and story featured in the chapters of your book.

This means that they can absorb the lessons you have distilled into words in *their* own space and time.

It means they can take a piece of who you are – all that you have included in your book – into the most private space. And it means that YOU become a part of their life during the time they hold your book in their hands, flick through the pages, and think and feel because of your writing.

Following on from this, it is in my heart to remind you that writing a book is an extraordinary and powerful opportunity for you:

The opportunity to connect deeply with another human being,

The opportunity to touch a complete strangers' life in a meaningful way,

And,

The opportunity to become omnipresent where your heart, mind and soul influence the lives of people whom you have never met, and may never meet.

To grasp this opportunity with both hands (a nice expression for a writer!), focus on your reader while you are writing. Take some time to think – and perhaps write – about the following questions:

What pain are they facing in their life right now?

What are they yearning to do?

Which struggle is holding them back from their goals and dreams?

12: Write for your readers

What do they aspire for above all else?

What do they need help with that they don't know how to ask for?

What is the most important thing to them in their life?

And,

What do they need to know that will help them achieve their goals?

Meditating on the answers to these questions will assist you to tune into your reader. It will help you to see beyond yourself (because sometimes we can be impossibly hard on ourselves as writer) and focus on the state of mind your reader is in, be it lost, helpless, curious or determined. It will also help you to gain a clearer picture of where your reader is – both geographically and in their life. You will connect with they are in: are they married or single? Looking for a career? Starting a business? Focused on growing their business from six to seven figures? Starting a family? Searching for 'the one'?

And then, you can then set yourself a target to write the most *inspiring* book on that topic for that person – the book that ends all other books they've ever read on the topic (which IS possible!). You can then fire yourself up with determination as you work on writing a book that occupies the reader's mind long after they have read it. You want it to be one that they feel compelled to tell their friends, loved ones, clients, and bookshop owners about.

Keeping your reader in your mind as you write your book is also an effective way to improve the quality of your writing. I have witnessed this ripple effect many times both in my own writing process and the process of the hundreds of people I have supported to become authors. Simply by placing the attention on the person we are writing for, we unlock a *whole* new flow of writing!

Doing this turns the often-lengthy process of producing a manuscript from a university assignment into a motivational speech. It seems to remove the drudgery that first-time authors can occasionally feel when they realise they have 30,000 words to write before their first rough draft is finished and replace it with excitement. And, it reminds the aspiring author *why* they are writing the book in the first place: to change the lives of the people reading it.

I tend to produce more uplifting and interesting content when I have the reader in mind. Beyond this, it minimises the amount of time I spend with a stilted writing flow while working on my book because I imagine myself in a conversation with the reader when I am putting pen to page. I know that focusing on the person whose life I desire to touch in a meaningful way makes the act of book-writing a joyous one.

12: Write for your readers

I certainly applied this when I sat down to write *this* book.

I thought about what your biggest concerns about writing a book are. I considered your hopes and dreams and what the higher intention for your book might be (it's likely that you want to inspire and empower people while using your book to grow your business). And, I also reflected on the questions I have been asked the most frequently in my time as a writing trainer and book mentor.

And then I formulated the entire book based on that. I wrote to silence the voices that distract you from doing your great work, remove the roadblocks in the way of your literary masterpiece, and encourage you to realise just how valuable the message you want to share is and can be for the world once you let it out. I encourage you to do the same with *your* book: to use your book to serve people.

If you want to become clearer on who you are writing for – because perhaps you haven't yet given it any level of significant thought – then here are some questions to think about:

- What is their gender?
- What is their approximate age?
- Where do they live?
- What do they do for work?

- What is their approximate income level?
- What is their nationality?
- What is their top spiritual or religious belief?
- What is their most consistent goal in life?
- What is the biggest problem they are facing?
- What is the cause of their pain?
- What are they most afraid of?
- What do they dream of and want most?
- What does your book do for or help them with?
- What does your book share that they don't know about?

Don't worry if you don't know all these details yet, especially if you are just starting out in business. It can take time and experience to develop resounding clarity on this. Write down the answers you *do* have clarity on, and then set out on the journey of finding the rest until you can see the reader clearly in your mind. You will know you have connected with the reader when you can almost feel their physical presence as you write your book.

The following three questions will prove themselves to be an asset for you as you focus on writing for your readers:

What would I love to say to this person?

12: Write for your readers

How else can I explain this to help and inspire this person?

And

What else does this person need to know to master (x) skill or topic?

We often take our story and content for granted in our lives, and answering these three questions helps us to overcome this and to see what we can teach and share with others from the outside perspective. The questions help us to tap into our areas of unconscious competence and the information that we know so well that it is as natural as breathing.

You can also use these questions to help you expand on various areas in your book if you need an extra 10,000 words to 'pad' your book out for the reader. A book under 30,000 words can print quite small and feel more like a brochure than a substantial book. This is important if you want to establish yourself as a credible leader or influencer in your field.

By reading through your content and asking these questions as you put yourself in the shoes of the reader, you will be able to easily add in content to finish your book. In fact, you might find yourself amazed at how much you can expand on once you view your book from an outside point of view.

It also wouldn't surprise me if this triggers several creative ideas for you that will make your book that much better! Stories you've forgotten about will pop in to your mind, you'll think of checklists to include in the visual layout of the book, and ideas for new exercises to give to your reader will flow to you as you review your manuscript from this perspective.

Sidenote: I think it's important for me to say here that there *are* readers that are 'yours'. I don't know if you've ever noticed, but there is a WIDE range of books in any bookstore – and each one of them has their own target reader. From business books to crime fiction and self-help, each book has been written for that 'one' person who will love it (and you know I don't mean one in the literal sense!). I recommend that you do the same!

I often take a moment to connect with the heart of the people I'm writing for before I sit down to write. I picture them in my mind. I see their faces reading my book and their hands holding it. I think about what their deepest secrets and highest hopes are. And then, I get to work doing everything within my power to use my words to create a life-changing impact on them.

I care about the reader – and I know you do too, otherwise you wouldn't be willing to invest your time, energy and finances into writing a book.

I want them to see how magnificent they are. I want the women to fully comprehend how exquisite they truly are and the men to realise how much we need them in the world. I want the reader to believe that

12: Write for your readers

they deserve anything that they want. I want them to see that great things are possible for them, despite their circumstances. And I want them to have a transformational experience through reading my book. I want what I write to matter to the person: to help them solve problems they haven't been able to do on their own and let them know that I believe to my core in their ability and potential to live an extraordinary life.

I know it's possible, so why wouldn't I aim for it? That's the power of the written word: to share secrets to big results, to whisper truths into the mind of a perfect stranger, and to lead the reader on a journey where they find gold at the end of the rainbow.

So, when you write your book, focus on the end in mind: the reader.

Reflect on what you wish for them to have in their future. Focus on who they are, what they want and need. And then think about how *you* and all that you write in your book can help them to fulfil their dreams, whatever they may be.

13: Focus on your long-term vision

"Writing a book is an adventure. To begin with, it is a joy and an amusement. Then it becomes a mistress, then it becomes a master, then it becomes a tyrant. The last phase is that just as you are about to be reconciled to your servitude, you kill the monster and fling him to the public."

Winston Churchill

At times, the journey of writing a book will challenge you so much that you may temporarily lose touch with why you began. You might encounter days where you feel like throwing your computer out of the window, or throwing in the towel completely. You might exclaim, "I don't need to write a book anyway!" I'm certain that there are thousands of books that haven't made it to the shelf because the author didn't know how to overcome the obstacles they were faced with in the writing process.

People often look at my long list of published titles and assume that writing a book is something that I do in my sleep. There is an automatic assumption that because I've done it so many times, it must just 'happen' naturally for me without effort and that each book I write is easier to produce than the one before it. Oh boy, how far this is from the truth!

Every book I have written has challenged me in a different way like none of the others before it did — and *yes*, that includes the one that you are reading right now. I've encountered moments where I wondered why I was writing the book, times where I thought my writing was pure crap (or downright boring), and moments where I didn't feel qualified or inspired enough to pull off the message I wanted to share with the world. I've felt like walking away, felt like I didn't deserve to publish it, and even questioned why I published it after I was holding it in my hands (shocking, perhaps, but true for at least one of my books!).

I often push myself to produce new and interesting content in my books. This fact alone means that I am continually questioning what my *real* next message is that I want to share. As you can imagine, this often sends me off on trips down the introspective rabbit

13: Focus on your long-term vision

hole in search of the best way to say something, or indeed, the best thing to say. Sometimes my grand plans for my books don't always turn out the way I originally envisioned or perhaps fantasised that they might. And so, there is certainly an abundance of challenge in my own book-writing process at times!

But what has been common to the growth process I have experienced with all of my books is that each one offered me the opportunity to become *more* of who I am. I have no doubt that the same will be true for you as you embark on your book writing journey. I know it will stretch you. In which way? Only the heavens or perhaps your soul knows that. What will you break through by persisting with your writing process? That is a gift that only you can discover (and it is a gift designed for you and you only).

The key to supporting yourself on this journey is to do just that: *support yourself!*

Too many aspiring authors are overly hard on themselves while writing, criticising their book before it's even written, and putting pressure on themselves to make it 'perfect' the first time around. They think that they should have mastered the art of rocking worlds with words before they've even really begun writing the first rough draft of their book.

Well, let me say this (and make sure that you *really* hear this on every level of your being!): *no* author writes a flawless manuscript on their first run.

Many of the best books – especially the classics – underwent not just one, but many drafts and versions before the title was published and declared ready for the readers. Significant time often goes into refining books before they hit print. Even though I wrote my fourth book, *The Inspirational Messenger*, inside of four days, I spent another six months letting the dust settle and adding 8,000 more words to the manuscript and tweaking what I had downloaded during my writing frenzy.

Without me telling you this, you might have just assumed that the best-selling authors of this world are just 'better' writers than you – and I can't have that, as the book within you may be the next big thing on the shelf; the next book the world is ready for and can't stop raving about.

This is why it is CRUCIAL that you support yourself *every step of the way* as you fulfil your dream of holding your book in your hands for the first time before sharing it with your readers. I am certainly not against you challenging yourself to produce a book that is worth its weight in gold – in fact, if that type of conquest inspires you, then go for it. But if you are crushing yourself under the weight of trying to write an A-grade piece of work the first time you write a book, and it's stopping you from writing, then perhaps this isn't the most effective approach!

13: Focus on your long-term vision

Through all the wisdom I have already shared with you in this book, there is one great secret to fulfilling your aspirations as an author. Here it is:

Stay focused on your long-term vision.

I can promise you that keeping a deeply inspiring and heartfelt vision in mind as you write your manuscript will be your greatest ally on the journey, followed closely by the team you surround yourself with as you write your book (you don't have to do this alone and I don't recommend that you do).

Reminding yourself of your dream each time you sit down for your precious, allocated writing time will give you the persistence you need to work through the sticky points in your book – like deciding chapter titles, how to say something, or working out where something should go. It will provide the determination to push through when the process seems to drag on forever like a road going nowhere.

A strategy to help with focusing on your long-term vision (or even just the bigger vision!) is to have the cover of your book designed early in the writing process. Even if it is just a mock-up of the final design, I have found that this simple idea always provides endless inspiration and yes, occasionally motivation, to those brave individuals who are embarking on the mission of writing a book.

I have used this strategy with almost all my own books. I finalise the cover design either right at the beginning of starting the manuscript or when I reach the 20-30% mark in the writing process. I then take a print-out of the book cover (typically just the front cover) and stick it on the wall in my office in a place where I can see it easily. In most cases, I keep it there for as long as it takes to finish my book and, sometimes, right up until I am holding the actual book in my hands.

This strategy is powerful as it trains your conscious mind to focus on the product you are producing, while also engaging your unconscious mind in the creation process. You can use your book cover for creative visualisation, imagining yourself holding the book in your hands. Or, in a more grounded way, you can use it to generate pre-sales or early interest in your book: a sure-fire way to make sure you don't give up on your writing process!

To implement this strategy, it is essential that you have clarity about the following aspects of your book:

- Title
- Subtitle
- Your author name (easy!)
- The genre
- The topic
- The main message
- Your target reader/audience

13: Focus on your long-term vision

- The symbolism/imagery for the cover
- How the book fits with your brand
- The colours for the cover design
- The approximate word count (for trim size)

You will also need a professional author headshot for the back cover and your one-line author bio (have a look through some of the books on your shelf to get some inspiration).

The reason you need clarity on the above is two-fold. Firstly, the graphic designer or designers you work with are likely to ask you about many, if not all, of these components. And secondly, you want to avoid having to redesign your cover from scratch at a later stage if you are halfway through writing your book and need to change the appearance of your book completely.

I hope it goes without saying that the cover for your book WILL be a crucial element of its success. Just ask any bookstore owner, agent or publisher and they'll tell you that people will even avoid buying a book with a low-quality cover unless someone else they know has *raved* about it. And so, the cover is not a part of your book you can afford overlook the details or shortcut. *But,* if you are clear on what the design will be – and you can see a clear enough vision of the perfect cover for your book – then YES, go ahead and have it designed to fuel you throughout your writing process!

It is also important to celebrate your small wins along the way: *every* bit counts towards your end goal of becoming an author.

Even adding 500 words to your book on a single day is progress worth acknowledging. I track my word count at the start and end of each writing session for the sole purpose of patting myself on the back! Remember that every word that you put into your book document counts and that sentences add up faster than you think – especially when you are in the 'write' state of mind!

Give yourself all the encouragement you need to bring this book that you dream of writing to life, even if that encouragement is twice or three times the amount you originally thought you might need to get the job done. Be patient with yourself as you resolve your problems surrounding and related to the book, for example, what the main message of your book is, how you are going to profit from your content, or who your target reader is. Stick with yourself from the first to the very last page of the book.

Hold the vision for your future and the picture of your life that you desire close to your heart as you write and *dare* to dream of what will become possible when the vision for your book becomes your everyday reality.

Conclusion

"If there's a book you really want to read, but it hasn't been written yet, then you must write it."

Toni Morrison

Through every twist and turn that your book writing journey holds for you, remember to focus on two things above all others:

1. **WHY you are writing the book,** and
2. **What you want the reader to get from the book.**

Keeping these two focal points in the forefront of your mind each day will help you to persist through every word, sentence and paragraph of your manuscript until the moment where you can throw your fists in the air and yell, "I'm finished!!" They will be a source of inspiration in times where your ink well has run dry. In times where you feel like giving up, they will remind you of the purpose of this book: to transform lives and to establish a thriving career simply by being YOU.

Once you are armed with rough draft in hand, the publishing process will be the next step on your path towards becoming an author. This journey of turning the Word document you have spent many hours becoming closely acquainted with into a finished, published title will also require your careful attention, patience and good old TLC. So, be prepared to keep on loving your book long past the moment where you gleefully punch in the final full stop.

The most exciting part of your journey as an author begins the moment the book is finally in your hands: the part where you get to experience and witness just how influential and life-transforming your words can be for other people. It's where you open yourself up to the world, build relationships with strangers, and become seen for all that you truly are.

It's important that you *celebrate* your immense accomplishment of bringing the book within you out with not just one, but *many* book launches. Honour the book that you have dedicated yourself to so diligently by making sure that it reaches the hands of many: the hundreds, thousands or even millions of people who are and have been waiting to read it.

Conclusion

And, finally, thank yourself for being one of the extraordinary individuals who chooses to step up and claim their place in ISBN history.

I look forward to reading your book soon.

With inspiration,

Emily Gowor

Enrol in Retreat To Write!

Would you love to write your book on holidays?

Ready to achieve your goal of becoming an author?

Want to use your book to grow your business?

Retreat To Write with Emily has been designed as the perfect time, place and way for you to get the book within you, out.

This full immersion writing retreat is more than a practical process of writing a book – it is an EXPERIENCE you will walk away from feeling deeply inspired!

You will come home after the retreat with a significantly progressed or completed manuscript – and a heart and mind full of vision, power and purpose.

For more information, log on to:
www.emilygowor.com

About The Author

Emily Gowor is a multiple published author, inspirational keynote speaker and writing trainer.

Emily facilitates writing retreats and private mentoring to help aspiring authors publish their story, content and message in a book. Devoted to seeing people find and fulfil upon their greatest aspirations, Emily overcame depression at age 19 to build a profound and thriving career bringing writing and inspiration to the world.

As the author of several books including The Write State of Mind, The Search For Inspiration, The Book Within You, The Inspirational Messenger and Transformational Leaders – Emily produced an award-winning blog, Life Travels, attracting thousands of readers. Emily was an editor on Dr. John Demartini's international best-selling book Inspired Destiny: Living a Fulfilling & Purposeful Life, and shared the stage with Dr. Demartini in 2015.

Having already made a difference in the lives of thousands before age 30, Emily continues to bring her brilliance and love for humanity to the forefront into all she does.

www.emilygowor.com

Acknowledgements

In expressing my gratitude for those who have contributed to this book, I would first love to thank the six participants who attended my first writing retreat and who journeyed with me as I produced *The Write State of Mind*. To Dannii Orawiec, John Pavone, Sharyn Bailey, Jo Worthy, Ally Pinnock and Kavitha Vipulananda, thank you for accompanying me as I brought this book to life.

Next, I would love to thank my partner Chris for being an endless pillar of strength and support for me in my life. Thank you for being the man by my side as I pursue my mission to bring inspiration and books to the world.

I would also love to express my heartfelt thanks to Rae Antony, the most extraordinary mother I could have ever wished for. Your love, patience, and shared inspiration for my mission brings me joy daily. Thank you for reviewing the book and helping me to polish my message for all the aspiring authors out there. It is truly a privilege to serve alongside you.

Thank you to my team at Gowor International Publishing for producing this beautiful book, and to Divine for the gorgeous cover design. Your work inspires me. And finally, thank you to all of the authors who have trusted me with their hearts, book ideas, and futures as I have guided them to achieve their goal of sharing their message on the page. Your messages matter to this world.

Additional Titles by Emily Gowor

The Book Within You: The Aspiring Author's Guide To Bringing The Book Within You Out, is an informative and insightful book on how to write a book and become an author.

Packed with years of Emily's experience of producing manuscripts, this book will guide and inspire you to bring the book within you, out.

The Inspirational Messenger: The 5 Pillars To Becoming Inspirational In Everything You Do is Emily's fourth published book. Written in just four days through inspired channelled writing, this book will touch your heart deeply and guide you to feel the presence of your soul so that YOU can become inspirational in the world.

www.emilygowor.com

www.ingramcontent.com/pod-product-compliance
Ingram Content Group UK Ltd.
Pitfield, Milton Keynes, MK11 3LW, UK
UKHW021258180426
11947UKWH00015B/911